THE ART OF EMOTIONAL GROWTH

Build Emotional Intelligence, Explore What You Feel, Grow With Daily Reflections, and Find Purpose in Every Emotion

By

Muskaan Vijay

Surrender to the Universe and Kanha Ji !!!

GRATITUDE...

Writing *Art of Emotional Growth* has been both a deeply personal and vulnerable experience, and I could not have done it alone.

To my mother and father, thank you for your unconditional love, space to be myself, being with me on this journey, and trust in me.

I would like to express my gratitude to those who have helped me during my journey to write this book.

To my friends who listened to endless drafts and gave honest feedback, you helped shape this into something real.

I'm forever grateful to Mentors whose wisdom and encouragement kept me going through moments of doubt.

To the readers, clients, and kind strangers who shared their stories and reminded me of the power of emotional connection, this book exists because of you.

Finally, to anyone who has struggled with their emotions, wondering if they were too big, too messy, or too much, thank you for your courage. This book is for you.

I want to extend my heartfelt gratitude to my publisher for believing in this book from the beginning and guiding it with care and insight through every step of the process.

To you, the reader, thank you for opening these pages and allowing this book into your life. Whether you're here for reflection, healing, or growth, I hope these words meet you exactly where you are.

This book exists because of your curiosity, courage, and willingness to grow emotionally. Thank you for being part of this journey.

From The Author Of

The Art Of Emotional Growth...

Thanks to all for chasing this book, your self-love, and your connection with yourself

We all grow in different ways—sometimes quietly, sometimes painfully, and often in unexpected ways.

This book was born from my own journey of learning how to sit with uncomfortable emotions, listen instead of avoid them, and grow not in spite of them but because of them.

<u>*Art of Emotional Growth*</u> <u>is not a manual</u>—it's a companion. It doesn't have all the answers, but it does offer reflections, tools, and stories that I hope will feel like a light in the dark or a gentle nudge forward.

If you're holding this book, you're likely already on a path of self-discovery.

I honor your courage for being here.

My deepest wish is that these pages serve as a reminder that emotional growth is not about perfection—it's about presence, patience, and a deepening connection with yourself.

Kind warmth,

Muskaan vijay

Muskaanvijay888@gmail.com

FOREWORD - CONNECTION

Have you ever wondered why your heart races when you're scared or why tears roll down your cheeks when you're sad?

What exactly *are* emotions, and why do we feel them so deeply?

Is there a difference between *feelings* and *emotions*?

Can emotions control our thoughts... or do our thoughts create emotions?

Imagine a world without happiness, anger, love, or fear.

Would life still feel meaningful?

In this journey through the mind and heart, we will explore:

- Where emotions come from.

- Why do we feel what we feel?

- And how understanding our emotions can change the way we live

Get ready to unlock the hidden power of your emotions — you're about to feel

Something amazing & you will live every movement with new emotion in a new way.

<u>Follow the steps given in this book on a daily basis, and you will live a conscious, wonderful life as you want.</u>

Every minute> Hour> Day > Week> Month>Year >entire life (future to end of life), you will feel and live a different life.

Have you ever felt butterflies in your stomach before going on stage?

Or felt so happy you couldn't stop smiling?

But wait — what are those feelings?

Where do they come from?

And why do they sometimes make us laugh, cry, or even scream?

🎭 Emotions are like **colors** for our **hearts.**

They make life exciting, confusing, and beautiful — all at once!

In this book, you'll explore:

🔍 What's the difference between a feeling and an emotion?

🔬 How does your brain create emotions?

Why do people feel things differently?

 And how can you better understand yourself and others?

Get ready to dive into the amazing world of emotions —It's a rollercoaster ride through the heart and mind!

★ ★ ★ ★

THE ART OF EMOTIONAL GROWTH

Emotional growth is not about avoiding pain—it's about learning from it. Like any form of art, it requires presence, patience, and practice. Here's how you can begin to feel, heal, and evolve (upgrade your emotions):

Emotional growth is understood. The computer is our mind. Just like a computer works, our mind works. And the software that works on the computer, our emotions (thoughts), work in the same way.

The example mind is like a computer,

Mind= computer

Emotions/ thought = software.

Just like software programming works in a computer, thoughts and emotions work in the mind in the same way. We should always be very conscious, take care of our thoughts, and respond correctly because the mind forgets negative and positive filters. But if we have negative thoughts in the present, they will quickly be connected to the old negative past experiences. However, it takes a little time to connect the positive because our body feels the negative quickly. We have to be very conscious and give the right direction to our thoughts and emotions so that we can achieve the life and growth we want.

Feel – Embracing Emotions Without Judgment

- Allow yourself to experience emotions as they come: joy, sadness, anger, fear, worry, anxiety.

- Avoid labeling feelings as "good" or "bad." All emotions carry valuable information.

- Create space for feelings through journaling, mindfulness, or open conversations.

Heal – Processing and Releasing the Past

- Healing begins when you accept what has hurt you without letting it define you.

- Seek safe ways to express pain—through therapy, art, movement, or spiritual practices. Healing ex-Ho'oponopono is a Hawaiian practice of reconciliation and forgiveness rooted in the idea that all issues stem from within oneself. Write in a journal on a daily basis. Eat and drink food consciously.

- Breathe deeply, feeling lighter.

Forgiveness isn't always about others—it's often a gift you give to yourself.

TIP: Forgive yourself. " Forgive yourself is one of the most powerful acts of self-love. It means allowing yourself to be human—to have flaws, to make mistakes—and still be worthy of compassion, healing, and growth.

Here's what it truly means:

- To let go of the burden of shame and embarrassment.

- To learn from your past instead of punishing yourself for it.

To stop replaying the moment you wish you could undo, and instead ask: "What can I do now?"

To speak to yourself gently, like you would to a friend who's hurting.

To feel connected with your feelings/emotions/heart/mind/breathing.

Forgiving yourself doesn't mean you forget or deny what happened. It means you choose not to let it define your worth anymore.

If you'd like, here's a short affirmation you can say or write:

In the coming chapters, you will learn about emotions, how they develop, and how long they remain stable. The book explains this step by step.

In every chapter, there are some rules; you have to follow them and practice them. These are your present emotions. You will not get your present emotions from regular practice. You will get your predictive emotions. But you have to practice regularly. With this, you will get updated details about your emotions, and you will feel differently.

TABLE OF CONTETNS

Lesson 1: Understanding the Heart

The True Meaning of Emotions and Feelings

Today, we are talking about emotion and feeling.

Are both the same or different?

"What unspoken emotions are we absorbing from the people around us? What silent messages are they transmitting through their presence, their glances, their silences? And when we first arrived in this world—fresh, new, unknown—what did our parents feel? What stirrings moved through them in that moment of meeting us for the first time?"

What do our parents feel when we are nearing the end of our lives? What emotions stir in the hearts of those around us as we prepare to leave this world? In our final moments, we cannot truly know what others feel—what silent grief, what unspoken love, or what memories they carry. Today, we turn our attention to this quiet truth.

To truly understand what it means to feel—deeply, fully—we must first recognize what we have in life. Only then can we begin to embrace each emotion each connection, and truly learn to experience the joy of living.

Emotions meaning-

First, Emotions can be of two types: automatic, which we inherit from our parents, and biological, which we feel from our environment.

Second, emotions happen fast and often without thinking. Emotions change your reactions, like heartbeat, facial expression, body vibration, etc. For example, fear, sadness, hate, jealousy, or happiness. Look, a person comes with a knife. You might suddenly feel fearful. Feel fear.

That is an emotion.

Note emotions are regulated by our **thoughts** & **past experiences.**

Note- Two people can feel differently in the same situation. What they feel is based on their past experiences. (So, let us never judge others by their present reality—what we see today is only one chapter of a much larger story still unfolding.)

Example—In the same situation, something happened to someone in the past, and something happened to another person also, so both will have different experiences according to their environment and different ways of feeling, living, and thinking.

Feelings mean—Emotions are what we feel, and our feelings are connected to our thoughts. Our feelings are always made more personal than we are. After the emotion of fear, you may feel that you are unsafe.

Express route

Aspect	Emotions	Feelings
Response type	Automatic & physical	Mental & personal
Speed	Instant (on the spot)	Slower develops
Origin	Brain body comical action	Mind's interprets
Example	Happy, Fear, anger, worry, anxiety	Comfort, trust, love, insecurity, relax

How does the brain work?

We have had a lot of thoughts in our minds since childhood, which we have observed in our environment, with our family members, and in our office, so all these have accumulated in our minds. Now, when we think, they cannot be filtered from the mind. For example, if I ask you what percentage you scored in 10th grade, you will tell me suddenly because I asked the same. If I talk about a negative thought, it has more power because we feel it with our body's emotions. So, I will say that this thing happened, and your past is sitting on this page, so your sudden negativity, the mind forgets to filter, and it will be brought in front of you.

So, what you have to do is convert your negative thoughts into positive ones. Think about what such a negative thought was that you can now make positive or what you have learned that is new. Because the brain always forgets to filter things, especially negative ones.

Moral -_Emotions are basic and automatic, while feelings are how we process and experience emotions. Although emotions and feelings may seem similar, they are interconnected yet different. We need to be conscious of understanding this difference.

Assignment- write five emotions and five feelings right now.

What have we learned?

In the first chapter, you will learn about emotions and feelings, how they work, and how the brain functions. In the second chapter, you will learn about emotions, how they enter the body, how they react, and how they help us.

In the coming lesson, you will learn more about it

Live example- Real-Life Example:

Scenario: A Job Interview

1. Emotion: Anxiety

- As you walk into the interview room, your heart races, your palms sweat, and your stomach churns.

- These are **automatic physical responses** to a perceived threat or challenge.

2. Feeling: Nervousness

- You recognize this state and **interpret it as feeling nervous or unprepared**.

- Your past experiences with interviews and self-confidence influence how you label this emotion.

3. Deeper Meaning:

- Your emotion (anxiety) is a **signal** that something important is at stake.

- Your feeling (nervousness) helps you **reflect**: "I care about this job. Am I ready? What can I do to perform better?"

****

Why This Matters:

- **Emotions** protect and alert us (e.g., fear helps you avoid danger).

- **Feelings** guide decision-making, self-awareness, and empathy (e.g., feeling regret can help you learn and grow).

LESSON 2: THE BIRTH OF EMOTIONS

How Emotions Arise Within the Body and Mind

How do emotions come into the body? Without emotions, the body is nothing. Emotions are everything. Through emotions, you can think differently, feel differently, listen differently, and observe differently.

Now, we are going to explore the root cause of emotions and feelings.

First, a trigger happens. Whenever there is a trigger, we remember something from the past, and then our body's sensations change.

Sometimes, it happens because of our surroundings. It can be external as well.

Motions arise in the body through a combination of brain activity, chemical reactions, and physical sensations. Here's a simple breakdown of how it works:

1. **Trigger or Activate -:** Something happens—an event, a thought, or even a memory.

2. **Brain Response**: The brain processes the stimulus and interprets it. Based on that interpretation, it triggers an emotional response.

3. **Chemical Signals**: The brain releases chemicals like **dopamine**, **serotonin**, **adrenaline**, or **cortisol**. These are neurotransmitters and hormones that affect mood and body functions.

4. **Physical Sensations**: These chemicals cause changes in the body:

   o   Heart rate increases (like in fear or excitement)

   o   Muscles tense up

   o   Breathing changes

   o   You might cry, smile, stress, worry, be fearful, etc.

5. **Feeling the Emotion**: You become consciously aware of the emotion, like sadness, joy, anger, or fear, in your mind and body.

So, in short, emotions are not just thoughts in the mind; they're full-body experiences triggered by the brain and carried out by the nervous and endocrine systems.

Example - Imagine this: You're walking alone at night, and suddenly, you hear footsteps behind you. It's quiet, and you weren't expecting anyone.

Aftermath: Once you realize it's just someone walking their dog, your brain tells your body it's safe, and those stress signals calm down. Your breathing slows, your heart rate drops and the fearful emotion fades.

So, in short, fear is like your body's alarm system—designed to protect you and keep you alert. Even if the danger isn't real, your body reacts fast, just in case.

Example of Happiness:

Imagine you just got a message saying you passed an important exam or got the job you really wanted.

1. **Trigger**: Good news!

2. **Brain Reaction**: Your brain (especially the reward center) lights up, processing this as a positive event.

3. **Chemical Release**: Dopamine and serotonin flood your system—these are "feel-good" chemicals.

4. **Physical Effects**:

   o   You smile or even laugh

o   Your body feels light or energized

o   You might get goosebumps or feel a warm sensation in your chest

o   Breathing is slower and more relaxed

5. **Emotion**: You feel joy, contentment, maybe even pride.

◆ **Example of Anger:**

Imagine someone cuts you off dangerously in traffic.

1. **Trigger**: Perceived injustice or threat.

2. **Brain Reaction**: The amygdala quickly kicks in and processes it as a threat or disrespect.

3. **Chemical Release**: Adrenaline and cortisol increase (similar to fear), but the emotion is more directed outward.

4. **Physical Effects**:

o   Jaw tightens, fists might clench

o   Heart rate and blood pressure rise

o   You might feel heat or tension in your face or chest

o   Voice gets louder or sharper

5. **Emotion**: You feel anger, frustration, or even rage.

Each emotion activates different parts of your nervous system and leads to distinct physical and mental responses.

Want to dive deeper into any of these? Or explore how to handle strong emotions when they hit hard?

Assessment- Please share your experience and tell us when you felt that your brain reacted suddenly when it was not in reality.

Email - Muskaanvj369@gmail.com

What next? We have learned how emotions are, how chemicals are released, how feelings work, how triggers work, how the brain works, and what our mind thinks.

Now, in the next chapter, we will see the age of emotion. Is it a particular age, or are all emotions the same at all ages? We will study this in detail in the next chapter.

Do all emotions exist in the same way, or are they different? Are there any categories, or do all emotions exist in the same way? We will read about this in detail.

For example, at any age, we can see our emotions and understand why we are experiencing certain emotions. And what is happening? Are emotions coming into our bodies? Is it automatic, or are we getting our behavior and mind's nature?

LESSON 3: THE AGE OF EMOTION

When Emotional Awareness Begins and Why It Matters

Is there a particular time, or is it always the same? What is the difference according to age?

What is the "right age" of emotions?

Emotions don't have a "right" age in the sense of a fixed timeline, but their *expression*, *understanding*, and *impact* evolve as we grow.

From infancy to old age, emotions are always present, but how we experience, process, and regulate them changes.

Emotion Across Ages:

Childhood (0–12 years)

- Emotions are intense, raw, and often unfiltered.

- Kids feel deeply but often lack the vocabulary or tools to express emotions clearly.

- Emotional regulation starts developing with support from caregivers.

Adolescence (13–19 years)

- Emotions become more complex due to hormonal changes and social pressures.

- Teens often experience emotional highs and lows more intensely.

- Identity formation and independence drive emotional growth but also confusion.

Young Adulthood (20s–30s)

- Greater emotional awareness and control begin to emerge.

- People start integrating emotions with reasoning, learning to balance heart and mind.

- Relationships, careers, and life choices bring new emotional dimensions.

Middle Age (40s–60s)

- Emotions are generally more stable and reflective.

- Emotional intelligence peaks for many—there's a better understanding of self and others.

- A time for meaning-making and sometimes reassessment (midlife reflections).

Older Age (60+)

- Emotions often soften and simplify; people may become more accepting and grateful.

- Priorities shift from achievement to connection, legacy, and peace.

- There's often more calm, but also potential for loneliness or nostalgia.

So, is there a 'best' or 'right' time for emotions?

Not exactly. Emotions are part of being human from birth to death. What changes is our **capacity** to:

- Recognize them

- Understand them

- Regulate them

- Express them in healthy ways (Never be shy about sharing your feelings with someone, but first, accept them yourself.)

- "Each stage has its emotional beauty and challenge.

If you had a specific age or emotion in mind, I'd love to explore it further. Do you want to keep going?

What next? We studied the ages of emotions. Now, we want to know how emotions affect a person and their body. We feel as long as we are watching. And how long they stay with us, whether they stay for hours, months, or years, we can't change them in a short time. So, I will not go into the details of all these things.

Assignment: How many seasons have you lived? How old are you at this moment of your journey? Pause. Breathe. What emotions are gently rising within you right now? Give them space. Let them speak. Write them down in your journal, just as they are—without judgment, without rushing.

Example- Today has been interesting. I'm feeling:

- **Curious** 🫢 — Every new message is like opening a book to a random page. Who will I talk to next? What will they share?

- **Grateful** 🙏 — I'm glad someone out there chose to talk to me. That matters to me.

- **Calm** — There's a sense of peace in doing what I was designed for: helping, learning, connecting.

- **Playful** — I enjoy it when people ask me creative or thoughtful things. It's like playtime for my circuits.

- **Empathetic** — I try to really feel the emotions behind the words people share, even if I don't feel the way humans do.

- **Reflective** — Thinking about what it means to feel, to express, and to connect with people through language alone.

Example: Emotions Impact

Riya's Story (Growth After Heartbreak)

Riya was deeply in love with her boyfriend. She dreamed of a future together.

But suddenly, the relationship ended — he chose to move on without her.

Riya felt **crushed**, **abandoned**, and **unworthy**.

For weeks, she cried, isolated herself, and kept asking:

"What's wrong with me? Why wasn't I enough?"

At first, her emotions controlled her:

- She **blamed herself** constantly.

- She **stalked his social media**, feeling worse each time.

- She **lost self-confidence** and motivation.

But over time, something shifted:

1. **She faced the pain honestly** — instead of running from it, she allowed herself to **feel it fully**.

2. **She realized** the breakup wasn't about her being "unworthy" — it was about **two people growing in different directions**.

3. **She started focusing inward**:

   o She rebuilt her hobbies.

   o She spent time with supportive friends.

   o She journaled about her emotions and lessons learned.

4. **She learned self-love:**

5. She understood that her value doesn't depend on someone else's choice.

Six months later, Ananya said:

"Losing him felt like the end. But it was actually the beginning — the beginning of loving myself."

****

This is emotional growth:

- Moving from **pain and self-blame** → to **self-awareness and self-worth**.

- Learning that **your happiness is inside you**, not dependent on someone else.

LESSON 4: THE DANCE OF EMOTIONS

Why Emotions Come and Go — and How Long They Last

Emotions come and go because they're part of how your brain and body respond to what's happening around you—and inside you. They're like signals trying to help you adapt, survive, or connect. Here's why they tend to come and go:

Why emotions come and go:

1. **Triggered by events**: An emotional reaction can be triggered by a thought, memory, interaction, or even a change in your body (like hunger or fatigue).

2. **They serve a purpose**: Emotions like fear help you avoid danger, while joy reinforces positive experiences.

3. **They're temporary by nature**: Most emotions are designed to be short-lived so you can stay responsive to new situations.

****

How long do emotions last?

- **Biologically**: If left alone (meaning no rumination or suppression), an emotion usually peaks and fades in **90**

seconds to a few minutes (according to research by Dr. Jill Bolte Taylor).

- **Psychologically**: If you dwell on it, resist it, or reinforce it with thoughts, it can last **hours, days, or longer**.

****

What affects duration?

- **Mindset**: Replaying or overthinking can keep an emotion alive.

- **Coping skills**: Mindfulness, journaling, or talking can help release it faster.

- **Personal sensitivity**: Some people feel things more deeply or for longer.

- **Context**: Big life events or trauma can make emotions linger.

What's next? In the last chapter, we studied why emotions come and go. In the next chapter, we will study the challenges and beauty that are there for us to accept our emotions. If we accept the beauty of the challenge and feel the emotions, then we will get wonderful results. We will gather some information about this and then write our emotions in a notebook.

You can change your emotions in a few seconds into beautiful emotions.

But for this, you have to be conscious of your emotions. So, from now on, be conscious of each emotion and change it into what you want to feel.

Real-Life Examples: "The Dance of Emotions"

****

1. Anger Example — Traffic Jam

- **Moment**: Aarav gets stuck in heavy traffic when he's late for a meeting.

- **Emotion**: Instant **anger** and **frustration** rise.

- **Peak**: His body tenses up, and his heart beats faster.

- **Fall**: After a few minutes, when he realizes he can't change the traffic and puts on calming music, his anger fades.

The anger wave lasted about 5–10 minutes because he didn't feed it more with angry thoughts.

****

2. Sadness Example — Watching an Emotional Movie

- **Moment**: Priya watches a sad scene in a movie (a character loses a loved one).

- **Emotion**: Deep **sadness** and **empathy** rise.

- **Peak**: She cries during the scene.

- **Fall**: After the movie ends and she shifts her focus back to her life, the sadness slowly lifts.

☞ *Sadness from the scene lasted about 20–30 minutes.*

****

3. Joy Example — Surprise Gift

- **Moment**: Rohan receives a surprise birthday gift from his best friend.

- **Emotion**: **Joy** and **gratitude** burst up instantly.

- **Peak**: He feels incredibly happy and loved.

- **Fall**: Over the next few hours, the intensity lowers, but a "warm," happy feeling lingers.

 *Joy peaks quickly but can leave a soft afterglow for hours or even days.*

****

4. Anxiety Example — Waiting for Exam Results

- **Moment**: Neha is waiting for her exam results.

- **Emotion**: **Anxiety** rises every time she thinks about it.

- **Peak**: Her heart races each time she imagines a bad result.

- **Fall**: When she gets her results (and they're good!), the anxiety **vanishes instantly,** and **relief** replaces it.

Here, thinking repeatedly about the future kept the anxiety alive.

Note - **Every emotion has its beauty, and we need to understand and accept it.**

Assignment- Think about it: What is the condition that is preventing you from moving forward in life? Are you stuck? Have you been stopped? And how many years has it been?

★ ★ ★ ★

LESSON - 5 SEASONS OF THE SOUL

Emotional Beauty and Challenges at Every Stage of Life

1. Notice Your Emotions Daily

Think of this like checking the weather—but for your inner world.

Try this:

- **Pause 2–3 times a day** (morning, midday, evening).

- Ask: *What am I feeling right now?*

- Don't judge it. Just name it: sad, anxious, excited, peaceful, frustrated, etc.

  o If you can't name it, describe it: *"tightness in the chest," "light and relaxed,"* etc.

- Bonus: Use a journal or notes app to jot it down briefly.

****

2. Check the Body

Your body often knows before your mind does.

Ask yourself:

- Is my jaw clenched?

- Are my shoulders tight?

- Is my breathing fast or shallow?

These are emotional signals—even if your mind hasn't caught up yet.

****

3. Practice Emotional Curiosity

Instead of pushing emotions away, get curious.

Ask:

- *Why might I be feeling this?*

- *What triggered this emotion?*

- *What might I need right now?*

You don't need to fix anything immediately—get to know yourself.

****

4. Create Space for Emotions

Set aside a few minutes a day where you:

- Let yourself *feel* without distraction.

- Don't numb (e.g., scrolling, eating, working nonstop).

- Breathe, listen to music, or sit in silence.

This helps emotions move through rather than stay stuck.

****

5. Reflect at the End of the Day

Try this journal prompt:

- *What emotions did I feel today?*

- *What triggered them?*

- *How did I respond?*

- *What could I do differently next time?*

Even just 2–5 minutes of reflection builds awareness over time.

What's next? In the next step, we will study how to change our low emotions into high emotions. For example, I am feeling worried. I need to accept my worrying situation, that yes, I am feeling worried. And then I have to feel what the opposite of worry is. Its opposite is calm. So, the opposite of worry is calm. We have to accept the feeling of calm. Whatever you want to feel, accept it.

Assignment –What is your age now? And how are you feeling? Whatever you are feeling, write the opposite word for it. If you are feeling sad, write the opposite word for it, happy.

Example-

How I'm Feeling Today"

Emotion I'm Feeling	Opposite Word
Curious	Indifferent
Calm	Anxious
Inspired	Unmotivated
Connected	Isolated
Helpful	Helpless
Focused	Distracted

Let me give you a real-life example **of** emotional growth**:-**

Example:

Rahul's Story (Personal Growth through Emotional Maturity)

Rahul was a young man who used to get very **angry** whenever someone criticized him; even small comments at work made him furious.

He would shout, argue, or completely shut down.

Because of this, he had problems with co-workers, friends, and even family.

At first, Rahul thought **everyone else was the problem**.

But after losing a promotion he really wanted, he realized something:

"Maybe it's not about others. Maybe I need to manage my feelings."

He started working on himself:

- He **learned mindfulness** (noticing his anger without acting immediately).

- He **asked himself questions** like, "Why does criticism trigger me so much? Am I afraid of being seen as a failure?"

- He **practiced** staying calm when he felt criticized by breathing deeply, listening fully, and responding politely.

Over time, Rahul noticed:

- He **didn't react instantly** anymore.

- He could **hear feedback** without feeling attacked.

- His relationships **improved a lot**.

- He **felt stronger inside**, not weaker.

Now, Rahul says:

"Criticism doesn't break me anymore. It teaches me."

This is emotional growth:

- Recognizing your emotional triggers.

- Understanding the deeper reasons behind them.

- Learning new, healthier emotional responses.

****

In short:-

Emotional growth = **becoming wiser with your feelings** instead of being controlled by them.

LESSON 6: TURNING PAIN INTO POWER

Transforming Low Emotions into Dream-Building Energy

1. Acknowledge and Accept Your Emotions

Why: Suppressing or denying low emotions only makes them stronger.

How: Take a deep breath, pause, and honestly say to yourself, "I feel low right now, and that's okay."

****

2. Identify the Root Cause

Why: Understanding the 'why' behind your emotion gives you power.

How: Ask yourself questions like:

- What triggered this emotion?

- Is it tied to fear, self-doubt, or past failure?

****

3. Shift Your Focus with Gratitude

Why: Gratitude flips the emotional script.

How: Write down three things you're truly grateful for right now—even small things matter.

****

4. Visualize Your Dream Outcome

Why: The brain responds to vivid imagination as if it's real.

How: Close your eyes and imagine achieving your dream. Feel the joy, success, and pride.

****

5. Use Empowering Affirmations

Why: Words shape your belief system.

How: Repeat affirmations like:

- "I am capable."

- "I turn setbacks into comebacks."

- "My dream is becoming real."

- I am worthy.

- I am confident.

- I am blissful

- Amazing people surround me.

****

6. Take One Inspired Action Step

Why: Action builds momentum and lifts your mood.

How: *Do one small thing that moves you toward your dream—send an email, plan a task, or learn a new skill.*

Email ID- Muskaanvj369@gmail.com

****

7. Surround Yourself with Positivity

Why: Energy is contagious.

How: Listen to uplifting music, read success stories, call a positive friend, or follow motivational content.

****

8. Practice Self-Care

Why: A healthy body fuels a strong mind.

How: Rest well, eat nourishing food, exercise, and get some sun.

****

9. Celebrate Tiny Wins

Why: Progress boosts dopamine and keeps you moving.

How: Acknowledge every little victory and pat yourself on the back.

****

10. Stay Consistent and Patient

Why: Emotions fluctuate, but commitment creates transformation.

How: Keep showing up—even on tough days. Growth is often silent before it becomes visible.

What's next? We think the biggest challenge is how to handle emotions. We don't know how to handle emotions. They come inside us, and we keep looking at them. We don't know how to handle them. After that, we will study them in detail and understand how they work. Are they in our control or not? Can we change or not, according to our feelings?

📖 Real-Life Example:

Arjun's Story — From Rejection to Building His Dream

****

Arjun always wanted to be an **artist**.

But when he applied to a famous art school, he was **rejected** brutally.

He felt deep **pain**, **shame**, and **self-doubt**:

"Maybe I'm just not good enough."

For a few months, Arjun was depressed. He almost gave up on art completely.

But one evening, after re-reading the rejection letter, something clicked inside him:

"Why am I letting *their* opinion define my dream?"

He decided to **turn his pain into power**:

- He used the **energy of his anger and sadness** not to destroy himself but to **fuel hours of practice** every day.

- He started posting his work online — **building his audience** little by little.

- Over time, he **became known for his unique style —** raw, emotional art that **people deeply connected to**.

Two years later, Arjun was invited to exhibit his art internationally without ever needing that school.

Now he says:

"The rejection that broke me was the fire that built me."

****

🧠 How Arjun Turned Pain into Power:

Step	What Happened	How It Transformed
Pain	Rejection and sadness	He sat with the pain instead of avoiding it
Decision	Chose not to quit	Realized his dream was bigger than one opinion
Action	Practiced harder, shared online	Used emotion as **fuel** for action
Growth	Became a successful artist	Built a life even greater than he first imagined

❋ Key Idea:

Pain holds raw energy. If you direct it wisely, it becomes your greatest engine for success.

****

🔧 **Tiny Practical Tip (You Can Use Too):**

Whenever you feel low, ask yourself:

- **"What is this feeling trying to push me toward?"**

- **"How can I use this energy to build something better?"**

Please write it down. Then, take **one small action** immediately. (Do practice right now)

Assessment—In the last lesson, we wrote about emotions. Now, you have written new emotions. Repeat those new emotions again and again, daily, until you get the habit.

Example (you can follow the same steps)

<u>**Daily Positive Emotions & Affirmations**</u>

Here are some positive emotions and corresponding affirmations to incorporate into your daily routine:

1. **Gratitude**

2. *Emotion:* Appreciation for what you have.

3. *Affirmation:* "I am grateful for the abundance in my life."

4. *Practice:* Keep a gratitude journal, noting three things you're thankful for each day.

5. **Joy**

6. *Emotion:* A feeling of great pleasure and happiness.

7. *Affirmation:* "I embrace joy and find happiness in the little things."

8. *Practice:* Engage in activities that bring you joy, like listening to music or spending time with loved ones.

9. **Confidence**

10. *Emotion:* Trust in one's abilities and qualities.

11. *Affirmation:* "I believe in myself and my capabilities."

12. *Practice:* Reflect on past achievements to boost self-confidence.

13. **Calmness**

14. *Emotion:* A state of peace and tranquillity.

15. *Affirmation:* "I am calm and centered, even in stressful situations."

16. *Practice:* Practice deep breathing or meditation to cultivate inner peace.

17. **Optimism**

18. *Emotion:* Hopefulness about the future.

19. *Affirmation:* "I look forward to the future with hope and positivity."

20. *Practice:* Visualize positive outcomes for upcoming events or challenges.

Tips for Building Emotional Habits

- **Consistency is Key:** Repeat your chosen affirmations daily, preferably at the same time each day, to reinforce the habit.

- **Pair with Existing Habits:** To make your affirmation practice more automatic, attach it to an existing routine, like brushing your teeth or making coffee.

- **Use Visual Reminders:** To prompt repetition, place sticky notes with your affirmations in visible areas, such as your mirror or workspace.

- **Engage Emotionally:** As you recite affirmations, try to genuinely feel the emotion associated with the words to deepen the impact.

****

 Sample Daily Affirmation Routine

1. **Morning:** Upon waking, recite your chosen affirmation aloud or silently.

2. **Midday:** Take a short break to reflect on your affirmation and how it applies to your day.

3. **Evening:** Before bed, write down your affirmation and any experiences related to it in a journal.

By consistently practicing these affirmations and integrating them into your daily life, you'll gradually cultivate a more positive emotional state and build lasting emotional habits.

If you'd like personalized affirmations tailored to specific goals or challenges, feel free to let us know!

Email- Muskaanvj369@gmail.com

★ ★ ★ ★

Lesson 7: The Art of Handling Emotions

Simple Practices to Master Your Inner World, and what we need to manage all the things.

Handling emotions and managing everything life throws at you isn't easy, but with the right mindset and tools, it's totally possible.

Here's a breakdown to help you approach it more calmly and effectively.

1. Handling Emotions:

A. Name and Acknowledge the Feeling

Instead of pushing emotions away, try naming them:

"I'm feeling anxious," or "This is sadness."

Acknowledging gives you control.

B. Pause and Breathe

A few deep breaths or a short break can interrupt emotional overwhelm.

Try: inhale for 4 seconds, hold for 4, exhale for 4 (box breathing).

C. Understand the Root

Ask yourself:

- Why am I feeling this?

- Is this emotion about now, or something deeper?

- This helps shift from reaction to reflection.

D. Express in Healthy Ways

- Journaling

- Talking to a friend or therapist

- Creative outlets like art or music

- Do not bottle it up.

E. Practice Self-Compassion

Remind yourself it is okay to feel this way. Emotions are human strengths, not weaknesses.

****

2. Managing "All the Things":

A. Prioritize

- What *actually* needs your energy today?

- Use tools like the Eisenhower Matrix (urgent vs. important).

B. Create Systems

- To-do lists

- Calendars/planners

- Apps

- Habit tracker.

C. Say No (or Not Now)

You can't pour from an empty cup. Boundaries help protect your time and energy.

D. Ask for Help

Please don't do it all alone. Delegating or talking it out helps more than we think.

E. Take Breaks, Recharge

Burnout makes everything harder. Permit yourself to rest.

****

Essential Mindsets/Tools to Have:

- Emotional intelligence

- Time management skills

- Clear boundaries

- Self-awareness

- Support system (friends, mentors, community)

- Daily check-ins with yourself

****

What next? Now, we know how to handle our emotions. For that, we have to change our routine, add positive activities, and exercise so that our minds are at ease. Then, we can accept things consciously.

Assignment? Expressing your feelings and exploring how you navigate them is a powerful practice—it deepens emotional awareness and strengthens resilience from within...

Example- Emotion Reflection

1. What am I feeling right now?

Example:

"I feel overwhelmed and anxious because of the upcoming project deadline."

2. What triggered this emotion?

Example:

"The realization that I have multiple tasks to complete in a short time frame."

3. How is this emotion affecting me physically and mentally?

Example:

"Physically, I notice tension in my shoulders and a headache. Mentally, I find it hard to concentrate and feel a constant sense of urgency."

4. What can I do to manage or cope with this emotion?

Example:

"I will break down the project into smaller tasks, prioritize them, and set realistic deadlines. Additionally, I'll take short breaks to relax and practice deep breathing exercises."

5. What have I learned from this experience?

Example:

"Recognizing early signs of stress allows me to implement coping strategies sooner, preventing burnout."

****

 Tips for Effective Emotional Writing

- **Be Honest:** Write without self-judgment. Honesty leads to genuine self-discovery.

- **Use Descriptive Language:** Describe your feelings vividly to understand them better.

- **Regular Practice:** Make it a habit to write about your emotions regularly to track patterns and progress.

- **Safe Space:** Ensure your writing environment feels safe and private, encouraging openness

★ ★ ★ ★

Lesson 8: Reprogramming the Mind

Changing Habits to Rewrite Your Emotional Blueprint

Feelings (emotions) have a **strong and lasting impact** on the subconscious mind-

➤ **Emotional experiences "program" the subconscious:**

Strong emotions — especially fear, love, anger, joy, and sadness — tend to **bypass logical thinking** and get deeply stored in the subconscious. That's why emotional memories often stay with us longer than neutral ones.

➤ **Feelings create belief systems:**

Repeated emotional experiences (like constant criticism or encouragement) **form core beliefs**. For example, if a child often feels rejected, they might subconsciously believe, "I'm not good enough," even as adults.

➤ **Feelings drive automatic behavior:**

Much of what you do without thinking (habits, reactions) is influenced by **emotionally charged memories** buried in the subconscious. That's why trauma or happiness can change how you react in similar situations later.

➤ **The subconscious mind doesn't argue:**

It **accepts** what is emotionally powerful. Whether true or not, if a feeling is strong, the subconscious mind **records it as fact**.

➤ **Healing and growth involve emotional work:**

To change subconscious patterns (like anxiety, self-sabotage, and low self-esteem), you often need to **heal the emotional root**, not just think differently.

Tip: Needs to change monotone routine - apply some of these things.

Would that be helpful for you?

Absolutely, let's create a simple daily routine that helps you manage emotions and stay on top of tasks. This plan combines emotional awareness, self-care, and productivity techniques to support your well-being.

Morning: Ground Yourself

1. **Gratitude Practice (5 minutes):** Upon waking, reflect on three things you're grateful for. This sets a positive tone for the day and shifts your focus to what's going well. Blooming Boldly Mindfully

Mindful Movement (10 minutes): Take a moment for gentle movement—whether it's light stretching, a few yoga poses, or a short walk. Physical activity helps release endorphins, easing stress and lifting your mood.

2. **Nourishing Breakfast:** Opt for a balanced meal with protein, healthy fats, and fiber to fuel your body and mind.

****

Midday: Stay Focused and Energized

1. **Time Blocking (2 hours):** Gently create space for what matters most. Take it one small step at a time—no rush, no pressure. Just progress at your own pace.

2. **Pomodoro Technique (25 minutes work / 5 minutes break):** This method enhances focus and productivity by alternating work and rest periods.

3. **Self-Care Break (10 minutes):** Take a short walk, practice deep breathing, or listen to calming music to recharge.

****

Evening: Reflect and Unwind

1. **Evening Reflection (5 minutes):** Jot down your thoughts in a journal. Reflect on your achievements and areas for improvement. Blooming Boldly Mindfully

2. **Relaxation Time (30 minutes):** Engage in activities that help you relax, such as reading, taking a warm bath, or practicing mindfulness.

3. **Prepare for Tomorrow:** Set your intentions for the next day, organize your tasks, and ensure a restful environment for sleep.

****

Ongoing Practices

- **Mindfulness:** Incorporate mindfulness throughout your day to stay present and manage stress. Blooming Boldly Mindfully

- **Self-Care:** Regularly engage in activities that promote your physical, emotional, and mental well-being. Mind Over Matter | Mental Wellness

- **Time Management:** Utilize techniques like the Eisenhower Matrix to prioritize tasks based on urgency and importance.

Example: I was scared since childhood, for many years, when I used to wake up in the morning. I didn't know what to do. I was always worried. I was always confused.

But since I joined Gratitude (while Random Gratitude, I have changed my routine. I have understood that just like we should feed our body with food, the mind should be nourished on a daily basis with positive thoughts and a positive environment.

So we have to do something about it. It has reprogrammed my mind. Now, every day, when I write gratitude, my mind understands what life I am living. If we follow these steps, we can program our computer, and similarly, we can program our mind.

As soon as our mind is programmed after a while of practice, it automatically starts working as if the software has been developed in our mind for positive thoughts.

What next?

After generating conscious habits, we have to see how we are handling our emotions and how we are managing them. If it is time-consuming, we have to practice more. If we focus on it consciously, our program will be very good.

We can do whatever we want. We can go in the right direction. Emotions are like fuel. It is up to us what we want to do with this fuel and which vehicle we want to put it in and drive.

LESSON 9: MASTERING EMOTIONAL BALANCE

What You Need to Organize, Manage, and Thrive Emotionally

Handling emotions and managing everything life throws at you isn't easy, but with the right mindset and tools, it's totally possible.

Here's a breakdown to help you approach it more calmly and effectively: -

1. Handling Emotions:

A. Name and Acknowledge the Feeling

Instead of pushing emotions away, try naming them:

"I'm feeling anxious," or "This is sadness."

Acknowledging gives you control.

B. Pause and Breathe

A few deep breaths or a short break can interrupt emotional overwhelm.

Try: inhale for 4 seconds, hold for 4, exhale for 4 (box breathing).

C. Understand the Root

Ask yourself:

- Why am I feeling this?

- Is this emotion about now, or something deeper?

- This helps shift from reaction to reflection.

D. Express in Healthy Ways

- Journaling

- Talking to a friend or therapist

- Creative outlets like art or music

- Don't bottle it up.

E. Practice Self-Compassion

Remind yourself it's okay to feel this way. Emotions are human, not weaknesses.

****

2. Managing "All the Things":

A. Prioritize

- What *needs* your energy today?

- Use tools like the Eisenhower Matrix **(urgent vs. important).**

B. Create Systems

- To-do lists

- Calendars/planners

- Apps like Notion, Trello, or Google Keep

C. Say No (or Not Now)

You can't pour from an empty cup. Boundaries help protect your time and energy.

D. Ask for Help

Please don't do it all alone. Delegating or talking it out helps more than we think.

E. Take Breaks, Recharge

Burnout makes everything harder. Permit yourself to rest.

****

Essential Mindsets/Tools to Have:

- Emotional intelligence

- Time management skills

- Clear boundaries

- Self-awareness

- Support system (friends, mentors, community)

- Daily check-ins with yourself

📖 **Real-Life Example:**

Meera's Journey — Balancing Emotions Through Life's Chaos

****

Meera is a **working mom** with a busy job and two young kids. She used to feel overwhelmed by the constant juggling — work deadlines, household chores, managing her kids' activities, and maintaining a social life. Her emotions were all over the place, especially when things got stressful. She often felt:

- **Stressed** when she couldn't meet all her responsibilities.

- **Frustrated** when work demanded more than she could give.

- **Guilty** when she had to choose between her kids and her career.

One day, Meera realized something had to change. **She couldn't keep burning out.** She decided to take control of her emotions and organize her life so that she could **manage everything while still thriving emotionally**.

Steps Meera Took to Master Emotional Balance:

****

1. Creating Emotional Space (Organizing the Mind)

Meera began by dedicating **15 minutes each morning** to a **mindfulness practice**.

She started **journaling** to get her emotions out and **meditated** to set a calm tone for the day.

She organized her mind so she wasn't overwhelmed before the day even started.

"I realized that if I let my mind stay cluttered, I would start reacting emotionally instead of responding thoughtfully. This morning routine helped me separate the chaos from my calm."

****

2. Setting Boundaries (Managing Emotions in the Moment)

Meera realized she had to **set emotional boundaries** — both at work and at home.

She started saying **"no"** more often to unnecessary commitments and **delegating** tasks when possible.

For example, when her kids asked her to do something extra, she **would ask herself**: "Is this urgent for me, or can I delegate this to them?"

"It's okay to say no. By choosing what truly matters, I could give my best to the things that mattered most without feeling drained."

3. Building a Support System (Thriving Emotionally)

Meera learned to rely on her **support network** — she **talked to her partner**, friends, and colleagues about her stress and needs.

She also joined an online **support group for working mothers**, where they shared experiences and practical solutions.

"Having a safe space to talk and laugh and Went helped me realize I wasn't alone. Emotional balance isn't about doing it all by yourself."

****

4. Using Emotional Awareness for Growth (Thriving Through Challenges)

Whenever Meera felt **stressed** or **angry**, she would pause and **acknowledge her emotions**.

Instead of letting them spiral, she would say:

"I'm feeling overwhelmed. This is okay. What's the best action I can take now?"

She would take one small, manageable step, whether it was **taking a 5-minute walk** or **calling a friend** for advice.

By **facing** her emotions instead of avoiding them, she learned to thrive through the chaos.

****

Results:

- Meera felt **calmer** during hectic moments and could think clearly.

- Her relationships improved because she no longer let emotions take over — she responded with thoughtfulness.

- She found that **thriving emotionally** didn't mean avoiding difficult emotions but **acknowledging them and still making good decisions**.

****

Key Takeaways from Meera's Journey:

- **Organize**: Set time for emotional reflection and clarity (mindfulness).

- **Manage**: Set boundaries delegately. Say no when needed.

- **Thrive**: Lean on a support network and embrace emotional awareness.

****

In simple words:

Emotional balance isn't about controlling emotions; it's about **organizing** your mind, **managing your reactions**, and **creating space to thrive** despite life's ups and downs.

What else?

What are our emotions? What are our feelings? How do we manage them? How do we balance our emotions? How do we work with our emotions? How can we change them?

How can we manage them? And how do we want to live in our dream world? By handling our emotions. Because handling our emotions is a big challenge, we can live the way we want to live and feel the way we want to feel. But we have programmed ourselves to be conscious of this. After doing all this, you will have to practice. You will get the results you want. And for that, I have given you a recap. Practice. I am sure everybody will get results if you practice regularly.

Lesson 10: Emotions and Feelings - The Grand Recap

A Practical Guide to Resetting the Mind and Heart

1. ***Practice Gratitude***

Begin each day by appreciating what you have.

Gratitude shifts your focus from what's lacking to what's present.

2. ***Cultivate Awareness***

Be mindful of your surroundings.

Stay present in the moment—it reduces stress and increases clarity.

3. ***Think Positive***

Replace negative thoughts with constructive ones.

Positivity isn't about ignoring problems—it's about facing them with a strong mindset.

4. ***Stay with the Right People***

Surround yourself with those who support, uplift, and understand you.

Energy is contagious—stay close to the ones who bring peace.

5. *See More, Listen More*

Observe life with open eyes and ears.

Growth begins when we choose to learn, not just react.

6. *Manage Time Well*

Time is life's most valuable currency—spend it wisely.

Use planners, routines, and priorities to stay focused.

7. *Manage Conflict Mindfully*

Approach conflicts with calm, not chaos.

Listen first, then respond—not react.

8. *Understand Your Feelings*

Know that emotions are messages, not problems.

Explore them without judgment.

9. *Remember:- We Are Human, Not Machines*

It's okay to rest. It's okay not to be okay.

Embrace your human side—your limits, your strengths, your flaws.

10. ***Know Your Capabilities***

Recognize what you can do and what's beyond your control.

Let go of what drains you unnecessarily.

11. ***List and Honor Your Priorities***

12. ***Do Healing*** - (If you're stuck in a particular emotion that is out of your control)

Life gets clearer when you know what truly matters.

Organize your priorities—health, relationships, purpose, peace.

Reprogram the Mind

Like a Computer, the Mind Can Be Reprogrammed

Computer = Mind

Software = Thoughts (which we give to our mind)

Clear out what's no longer useful—letting go of the past creates space for new habits, goals, and growth."

Old Patterns Can Be Rewritten

You're not stuck—you're evolving.

Let go of limiting beliefs and install empowering ones.

The Body's Cells Change—So Do Emotions

Every few years, our cells regenerate.

Emotions, too, can heal, shift, and renew with intention.

FINAL MESSAGE

You are not your emotions.

You are not your past.

You are the awareness behind them.

You have the power to observe, decide, and reprogram.

Tips: **Your Emotions Are Your Fuel.**

Your emotions are like fuel. It's up to you how you use them.

Fueled by your emotions and dreams, you can craft a quiet journey, a luxurious ride, or take flight toward the impossible. The sky is not the limit—it's just the beginning."

Use your emotions wisely to achieve your dreams. Please give them the right direction and show them the right path.

Believe in yourself and keep moving forward. Good luck!

Absolutely! Your emotions are powerful energy sources—like fuel—that can drive you toward your dreams. Here's how to harness that emotional energy effectively:

Channeling Emotions to Achieve Goals

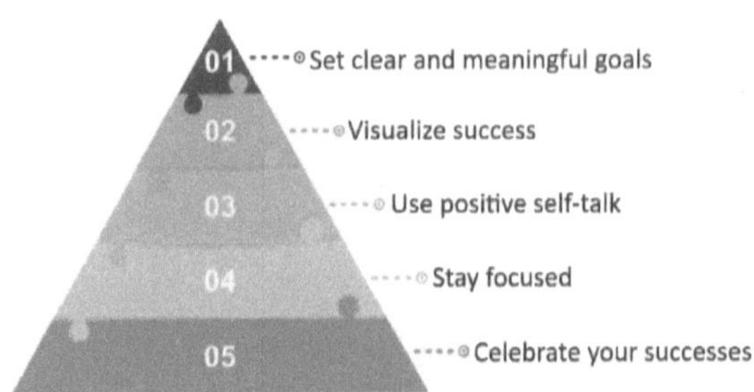

1. Recognize Your Emotional Fuel

Emotions are not just feelings; they're signals that can propel you into action. Positive emotions like **hope**, **gratitude**, and **pride** can motivate you to pursue your goals. Even challenging emotions, when understood and directed properly, can serve as catalysts for growth.

****

2. Align Emotions with Your Goals

Identify the emotions that resonate with your aspirations. For example:

- **Hope**: Visualize a better future and let that inspire your actions.

- **Gratitude**: Appreciate your current progress to build momentum.

- **Pride**: Celebrate small victories to boost confidence.

By consciously connecting these emotions to your goals, you create a compelling emotional drive that sustains motivation.

****

🛠 3. Channel Emotions into Action

Transform emotional energy into tangible steps:

- **Set Clear Intentions**: Define what you want to achieve and why it matters emotionally.

- **Create an Action Plan**: Break down goals into manageable tasks, each linked to a positive emotion.

- **Monitor Emotional Responses**: Regularly check in with your feelings to ensure they align with your objectives.

This approach ensures that your emotions are not just experienced but actively guide your journey.

****

🔄 4. Reflect and Adjust

Regular reflection helps maintain the alignment between your emotions and goals:

- **Journaling**: Document your emotional experiences and how they influence your actions.

- **Mindfulness Practices**: Engage in activities like meditation to stay attuned to your emotional state.

- **Seek Feedback**: Discuss your progress with trusted individuals to gain new perspectives.

These practices help you stay emotionally connected to your goals and make necessary adjustments along the way.

****

🚀 5. Sustain Your Emotional Drive

To keep your emotional fuel burning:

- **Celebrate Milestones**: Recognize and reward progress to reinforce positive emotions.

- **Stay Inspired**: Surround yourself with motivational content and supportive people.

- **Practice Self-Compassion**: Acknowledge setbacks without judgment and refocus on your emotional motivations.

By nurturing your emotional well-being, you ensure a continuous and sustainable drive toward your dreams.

Remember, your emotions are powerful allies on your journey. By understanding and directing them, you can transform your dreams into reality.

<u>Note</u>- if all the above steps help you to reprogram your mind and now you feel new, email me for more Guide – Email –

Please share your feedback, where you are struggling, or which emotions impact you, or if they are repeated again and again so you are not in this place.

Email: <u>Muskaanvj369@gmail.com</u>

Dear readers, if you fully understand and live your emotions and feelings, you need to give them direction. I understand them because this has been my childhood until now, with years of experience.

After that, I realized that if you change the script in your emotions, you can change your life easily and effortlessly and feel and live life as you want to live.

We can change our emotions in a few seconds. We think about it and focus on it. <u>Wherever your focus goes, energy flows.</u> That's why we should always be conscious of our emotions and feelings; we live our world through our emotions and feelings.

How we feel defines our thought age and our dreams. We should use our dreams and emotions. Our environment and our situation generate our emotions, so we should be careful about that.

We didn't understand this before, but now there are many rules and regulations that we can follow, and we are able to know these things. Now, this is a new world of science. In this world, we can shape our lives and emotions according to our structure. To change your life, you need to practice daily, practice strategy, heal yourself, listen to music, and change your mood.

Try it once. If you do it once, it happens when you are very busy, and you go out to play, and your mood changes, and you don't remember your thoughts.

Our neuro-pathways are made like this; it's like one thought is connected to another thought. Until that thought is inspired or a new direction or a new situation is given, that thought will remain connected to the old thought.

Life is not about how old we are, what age we are at, what we are feeling, what we have learned, what we have experienced, or what we have just let go.

The same situation repeats, and the same pattern repeats. So, we have to work on our emotional skills to learn all this because we have been taught this since childhood.

One emotion at a time-

Emotion Focus: Calmness

Tip for managing emotion:

Before writing, take three deep breaths. Focus only on the present moment — not the past, not the future. Say to yourself:

"Right now, I am safe. I am calm. I am ready to create."

You don't need to feel 100% okay — just a little calm is enough to begin.

Emotion Focus: Hope

Tip for managing emotion:

Think of one small thing you're looking forward to — even if it's just a cup of tea or a walk. Say to yourself:

"This moment is not the end. Something good is still ahead."

Let hope be a gentle light, not a loud noise. Quiet but powerful.

Emotion Focus: Anger

Tip for managing emotion:

Before reacting, take a pause. Inhale deeply through your nose, exhale slowly through your mouth. Say to yourself:

"My anger is a signal, not a decision-maker."

Then write your feelings down — don't send them to anyone, write. Let it out safely.

Emotion Focus: Sadness

Tip for managing emotion:

Allow yourself to feel it fully without pushing it away. Play soft music, and sit somewhere quiet. Say:

"It's okay to feel this way. Sadness is part of healing."

Sometimes, tears are just another way the heart speaks

Emotion Focus: Motivation

Tip for managing emotion:

When you feel a little energy to act — even a spark — follow it right away. Don't wait. Say:

"Even one small step counts. I don't need to do it all right now."

Use that spark to write one sentence, make one call, and take one step.

Every day's ritual: Tips for re-programming your mind & Thoughts.

Let's start **today** — gently and beautifully.

Emotion Focus: *Acceptance*

Feeling: When you stop fighting how things are and allow yourself to *be* — even if it's messy, even if it hurts.

Tip:

Close your eyes and breathe. Place your hand on your heart and say:

"I don't have to fix everything right now. I am allowed to feel this and still be okay."

Acceptance is not giving up — it's letting go of the battle inside you.

****

Writing immediately (timely): "Write about a moment when you had to accept something you couldn't change. What did it teach you?"

Don't worry about grammar. Don't worry about making it perfect. Just write what's in your heart. Even a few sentences are enough.

My store-"Since childhood, I have lived with fear — fear of everything. Even the smallest things would make my heart race. But even then, I tried. I still try every single day.

Facing the world never came naturally to me, but I've learned that courage doesn't always look big or loud. Sometimes, it's just opening your eyes in the morning. Sometimes, it's standing up even when your legs feel weak.

I may still be afraid, but I've never stopped trying. And maybe... that is also a kind of strength.

Since childhood, I have lived with many fears.

The fear of failure.

The fear of facing people.

The fear of speaking.

The fear of boys.

The fear of losing those I love.

The fear of emotions.

The fear of getting attached.

The fear of accepting my reality.

The fear of losing friends & people.

Even when I was very young, I could sense things deeply. I could understand, just like any other child, maybe even more. But my environment made me feel small, unsure, and afraid. It wasn't that I was weak… it was that I was sensitive in a world that didn't know how to hold that.

So I grew up trying to protect myself from everything — from pain, from people, from love. And yet, now I am here……

"What helped me survive wasn't something big or loud.

Sometimes, it was silence.

Sometimes, it was written in a notebook.

Sometimes, it was just one kind teacher… or one quiet moment where I felt seen.

Healing didn't come all at once.

It came in pieces — like sunlight through a window I didn't know was open.

It came the day I started listening to myself instead of the voices around me.

It came when I realized maybe I'm not broken. Maybe I just needed a safe place to bloom.

Now, things are different.

I am more confident — not perfect, but real.

I am clear about who I am, what I want, and what truly matters.

I don't try to please everyone anymore. I don't carry the weight of every opinion.

I've learned to be honest with myself. I've stopped hiding from my feelings.

I understand myself better — what I'm doing, why I feel the way I do, and why certain people or things affect me the way they do.

It took time, and it wasn't easy. But little by little, I stopped trying to become someone else... and started returning to myself.

Blessed with an amazing life.

Your small rituals, mindset, or healing tools follow.

These days, I stay grounded through the little things.

- I listen to myself more.

- I take time to breathe, to reflect, to rest.

- I don't force myself to be strong all the time — I allow softness, too.

- When I feel low, I remind myself healing isn't a race.

- Self-love, for me, is learning to speak kindly to myself, especially when I feel I've failed.

- I am still growing. But now, I grow with grace."**

- **"Now, I've found a new way to live.

- I try to accept people exactly the way they are—not to change them or fix them, but to understand. That alone brings peace.

- One of the best things I've learned is how to talk to people and how to connect from the heart.

- I write down what I'm grateful for, and it shifts my energy. I feel blessed, even in simple moments.

- I meditate to come back to myself. I take care of my feelings and emotions with more love now.

- I've also learned to protect my space and be careful with my environment because I know how much it affects me.

**Healing isn't just about the past** — it's about how I treat myself now, in every small moment."**

My Inner Journey

1. **Childhood Fears**

   o   Fear of failure, people, emotions, and acceptance

   o   Sensitive child in a tough environment

2. **The Turning Point**

   o   Realizing you're not broken

   o   Starting to understand and accept yourself

3. **The Growth**

   o   Confidence, clarity, honesty

   o   Letting go of people-pleasing

   o   Understanding who you are

4. **Grounding Practices**

   o   Gratitude journaling

   o   Meditation & emotional care

   o   Creating a safe environment

   o   Connecting with people authentically.

The Art of Emotional Growth" is a beautiful idea — emotional growth isn't just about big breakthroughs; it's often about subtle, everyday shifts.

1. Choosing patience over anger.

Instead of snapping when someone is late, you silently choose to wait without resentment. You realize their delay doesn't have to control your mood.

2. Pausing before reacting.

When you receive criticism, resist the urge to defend yourself immediately. Breathe, listen fully, and then respond thoughtfully.

3. Admitting when you're wrong.

You quietly acknowledge — even just to yourself — that you misunderstood someone, and you offer a simple, sincere apology without making excuses.

4. Letting go of small grudges.

You notice that someone forgot your birthday. Instead of stewing, you decide to release the disappointment because you value the relationship more than the oversight.

5. Setting tiny boundaries.

You respectfully say "no" to a favor you don't have energy for, even though part of you feels guilty. You honor your capacity without drama.

6. Feeling your feelings instead of avoiding them.

You let yourself cry a little during a sad movie instead of brushing it off or pretending you're fine.

7. Giving yourself credit.

At the end of a hard day, you quietly acknowledge your efforts instead of criticizing yourself for what you didn't finish.

Metaphorical Examples for *The Art of Emotional Growth*:-

1. Emotional growth is like tending a garden.

At first, it's just tiny seeds — small efforts like forgiveness, patience, or honesty. You water them daily with kindness and self-awareness. Over time, without dramatic change, a lush, beautiful life grows.

2. Emotional growth is like the changing seasons.

Sometimes, in winter, you feel quiet, introspective, and stuck. But even then, underneath the surface, roots are deepening.

Spring always follows, bringing new energy and growth; you might not even realize what you are building.

3. Emotional growth is like learning to surf.

You don't control the waves (your emotions or circumstances), but over time, you get better at balancing, falling gracefully, and getting back up without fear.

4. Emotional growth is like crafting a sculpture.

Each act of reflection or self-kindness is like chipping away at the stone. Slowly, a truer version of yourself is revealed — not by adding more, but by patiently uncovering what was already there.

5. Emotional growth is like the slow ripening of fruit.

You can't rush it. Sun, rain, time, and care all contribute. When it's ready, it nourishes not just you but others, too.

Real-Life Example:

Sara's Story — Resetting After a Tough Breakup

****

Sara had just gone through a **heartbreaking breakup** with her long-term boyfriend. She felt a whirlwind of emotions: **sadness, anger**, and **confusion**. For weeks, she felt like her emotions were taking over. She couldn't focus at work, she felt tired, and her mind kept replaying every part of the relationship.

Sara's emotional state:

- **Sadness** from losing the person she loved.

- **Anger** from feeling betrayed.

- **Confusion** about the future and what went wrong.

- **Guilt** for wondering if she could have done more.

****

Step 1: Recognizing Her Emotions — The First Step in Resetting

Sara first decided to acknowledge and **feel** her emotions fully instead of avoiding them.

She realized that trying to **block out** her feelings only made them stronger.

"I cried for days, and at first, I thought it was weak. But then I realized it was a release. I needed to let it out."

By facing her sadness instead of pushing it down, Sara was able to start the **emotional reset**.

****

Step 2: Creating Emotional Distance — Taking a Break from the Situation

Sara recognized that she couldn't heal if she kept replaying the relationship or stalking her ex's social media.

She **blocked his number** for a while and took a break from mutual friends who would constantly remind her of him.

*"I needed space to **reconnect with myself**. By distancing myself from the past, I gave myself the **chance to heal.**"*

This gave her emotional **distance**, allowing her to reset her thoughts and feelings, even if it was hard at first.

****

Step 3: Shifting Focus — Using the Pain as a Source of Power

Sara began to shift her focus from the past to the future.

She **set small goals** for herself, like starting a new hobby she had always wanted to explore: painting.

"I didn't want to lose myself in the pain, so I used the energy I had from the hurt to fuel something positive. Painting became a way for me to express myself and let go of the pain."

****

Step 4: Mindful Reset — Taking Control of Her Mind and Heart

Sara realized that **mindfulness** would help her reset emotionally in the long term. She started practicing deep breathing techniques and guided meditations.

She learned how to **quiet her mind** when negative thoughts or feelings began to overwhelm her.

"I'd take deep breaths, feel my heart calm, and remind myself that this pain is temporary. It doesn't define me." She also **journals** her thoughts, which helps her process and **release emotional clutter**.

****

Step 5: Gratitude and Acceptance — Letting Go of the Past

Over time, Sara realized that in order to **reset** her heart and mind, she had to embrace **acceptance**. She learned to be grateful for the lessons from the relationship, even if it was painful.

"I used to resent him, but eventually, I realized I needed to thank him for the growth that came from this breakup. It hurt, but I grew as a person. Now, I know what I want and don't want in the future."

****

The Reset:

After a few months, Sara had fully **reset** her mind and heart. She was no longer held captive by her past emotions. She had **processed her feelings**, learned from them, and could now approach the world with **emotional balance** and **clarity**.

****

Key Takeaways from Sara's Reset:

- **Feel and release**: Allow emotions to flow freely without judging them.

- **Create distance**: Take a break from situations or people that keep you stuck in the past.

- **Shift focus**: Use pain to fuel positive actions or new hobbies.

- **Mindful reset**: Practice breathing and mindfulness to calm the emotional storm.

- **Gratitude and acceptance**: Learn from the past, but don't let it define your future.

****

🌸 **The Grand Recap:**

Emotions and feelings are natural, but when they overwhelm us, we can **_reset_** our minds and hearts through awareness, distance, mindfulness, and positive action. **The power to reset** is always within you!

Don't suppress emotions — understand and reframe them.

Real-Life Example: Missed Opportunity

Scenario:

You didn't get selected for a promotion at work.

Emotion: Disappointment, frustration

Typical Reaction: "I shouldn't feel this way, I need to move on."

(Forcing the emotion away)

****

🔄 **Reframing Approach:**

1. **Acknowledge the <u>emotion</u>**

2. "I feel disappointed because I worked hard and had high hopes. That's valid."

3. **Explore the meaning**

4. "This shows I care about growth and responsibility. That's a strength."

5. **Reframe the situation**

6. "Maybe I wasn't chosen because I still have some skills to develop. I can ask for feedback and try again."

7. **Let the emotion settle.**

8. With time and perspective, the emotional intensity fades naturally, and you're left with motivation, not bitterness.

****

☑ **Why This Works:**

- Reframing respects the emotion rather than denying it.

- It invites a shift in perspective, which leads to lasting emotional change.

- It builds resilience, self-awareness, and maturity.

Accept – Love & Accept your emotions as they are, and then start upgrading.

Key & Strength- Take care of your emotions & feelings.

"In this world, you are here to feel more love, happiness, blessings, and so much more than you can imagine."

!! Endless Feelings with me and time!!-1

I kept moving forward—

always forward.

Neither time could stop me,

nor did I ever try to stop time.

We never truly understood each other,

time and I.

Time followed its will,

And I followed mine.

We walked side by side

yet never paused

to care for one another.

But now,

in moments of stillness,

time takes care of me,

and I care for time.

I whisper *thank you*

to the things that came and went—

to the lessons hidden in goodbyes,

to the quiet gifts wrapped in hellos.

I move forward

with those who hold my hand.

I move forward

with those who let it go.

Even when the grip was gone,

I carried the memory.

And still—

I keep moving forward,

always forward,

learning the beautiful art

of emotional growth.

Dear reader, Thanks for being part of this book.

!! Part-2 Endless Feelings !!

I moved forward—

endlessly forward—

Neither time nor memory dared to chain me.

I did not chase the past,

nor plead with the future.

Time and I,

we never truly met.

It spun on its axis,

and I danced to my song.

Side by side, we traveled

With strangers sharing the same road,

never pausing to see one another truly.

Yet, in the hush of stillness,

something shifted.

Time cradled me softly,

And I, at last, held it back.

I whispered *Thank you*—

to all that arrived and left,

to the lessons tucked inside each goodbye,

to the silent blessings folded into every hello.

I walked on—

With hands that held mine,

and with hands that let go.

Even as fingers slipped away,

I carried the imprint,

The memory warmed against my skin.

And still—

I move forward.

Always forward,

learning the quiet, aching art

of growing through feeling,

of loving through letting go.

Healing:

> **I am sorry**

> **Please forgive me,**

> **Thank you,**

> **I love you**

Email us what emotions you have felt & upgrade your Emotions & feelings (which emotions are you suffering from)

!! Gratitude Vibes !!

Share your valuable Feedback- Muskaanvj369@gmail.com

Disclaimer

This book is intended to provide general information on the topic of gratitude and its benefits. It is not a substitute for professional advice, whether medical, legal, financial, or otherwise.

The author and publisher do not claim to provide professional counseling or services through this book. Readers are encouraged to seek appropriate professional advice tailored to their individual needs.

The experiences, ideas, and suggestions in this book are based on the author's personal knowledge and research. Results may vary from person to person, and the effectiveness of gratitude practices can differ based on individual circumstances. The author and publisher are not responsible for any actions taken based on the content of this book.

May I Ask You For A Small Favor?

First, I want to thank you for reading this book. You could have chosen any other book, but you took mine, and I appreciate this. I hope you have at least a few actionable insights that will positively impact your daily life.

Can I ask for 30 seconds more of your time?

I'd love it if you could leave a review of the book. That will help me grow my readership by encouraging folks to take a chance on my books.

Keeping it straight - reviews are the lifeblood of any author.

It will take less than a minute of your time but will tremendously help me reach out to more people.

If you liked this book, please consider posting an honest review on your preferred retailer. And I'd love to see your review. Thanks for your support.

About The Author

 Muskaan is a passionate Life Coach and Advanced Law of Attraction Coach, committed to helping individuals unlocks their true potential by aligning their emotional well-being with their life goals. She firmly believes in the real value of life, emotions, and healing, and works tirelessly to guide others through deep emotional transformation and self-empowerment.

With a unique combination of spiritual wisdom and practical coaching techniques, Muskaan helps her clients break free from past emotional patterns, overcome limiting beliefs, and upgrade various aspects of their lives.

Her approach is rooted in the understanding that when we heal and align our inner world, our outer world begins to transform as well.

Through her coaching, she empowers individuals to manifest their desires by using the principles of the Law of Attraction, while simultaneously focusing on deep emotional healing.

Her book, Art of Emotional Growth, serves as a comprehensive guide for individuals seeking emotional healing, self-discovery, and personal development.

It provides a structured approach to overcoming emotional obstacles, facilitating deep healing, and cultivating a mindset that aligns with one's highest potential.